chance would be a fine thing

chance would be a fine thing

Anthony McCann

First Printing, 2012

ISBN 978-1-909016-01-9

First Edition

Clarion Publishing
PO Box 45298
London
England
SE10 1BN

www.clarionpublishing.com

Ordering Information
To order additional copies of this book (either in bulk or individual sales), please email **orders@clarionpublishing.com**, and give the title, author, and ISBN number, along with any additional details relating to your enquiry. We will be happy to assist you.

Cover design by Jeff Sheinkopf Design

www.jeffsheinkopf.com

For Emma

Table of Contents

Some clocks tock upon the wall

Some clocks tock upon the wall
But all mine does is tick
I sometimes think it learnt it wrong
I sometimes think it's thick

I'm sure that when I go to sleep
It always does it right
That malicious little clockface
Probably does it out of spite

But my mother says it's not for me
To judge when things are strange
It's not my fault my ticking clock
Is just that little bit deranged

Maybe it got all confused
While trying to work out Time?
Maybe my dysfunctional ticking clock
Is a budding Einstein?

Does it think that Time moves forward?
Does it think that Time moves back?
Is it static or elliptical?
Is it fiction or is it fact?

Is Time without form all fuzzy and warm?
Without shape is it squidgy and blue?
If Time had a date would it ever be late?
If it had legs would it live in the zoo?

Does it think that time's all broken up
Into minutes and hours and days
Or a continuous continuum
That continues in infinite ways?

Does it worry about quarks and quantum leaps,
Time-shifts and Schroedinger's cat?
Or would it swear to you over a pint or two
That it doesn't have a clue about that'

Maybe it's just the cogwheels
That aren't turning right at all?
Maybe it's got influenza
Or just caught the common cold?

Maybe some clocks are just made that way
Just unfortunate, not stupid or thick
Still, some clocks tock upon the wall
And all mine does is tick.

Border

The cold in-between
Of a thousand somethings and nothings
That make us what we are
And what we are not
One on the other side
Looking back over the line
In the sand
The hedge
The ditch
The cold comfort of a line well travelled
But never quite as human
As the walk along the wall.

I met a woman last week
Whose grandmother lived in five different nations
Even though she never left
The wee cottage where she was born.

A strange way to live some might say
But not quite as strange as the
Pen-and-papered filing cabinets
In which were registered
Her many locations
The lie of ages
The cold in-between
Of a thousand somethings and nothings
That do not really make us what we are.

Untitled

Will do
Going to
Am doing
Did.

Will do
Going to
Am doing
Dead.

Wanting

Sometimes I forget
I don't have to
Do what I want
Say what I want
Get what I want
Achieve what I want
Eat what I want
Buy what I want
Live where I want
Have what I want

Sometimes I forget
There are times when
I'm not sure what I want,
Even as I want it

Sometimes I forget
What I want
May not be what I want
But what other people want me to want
And I never noticed that I was
Thinking their think
Speaking their speak
Doing their do

Sometimes I forget
If what I want isn't here
Then being here isn't what I want
And I'm only ever going to be here.

Sometimes I forget
What I want
May not be helpful

Sometimes I forget
What I want may be
Planted by the fixer
Nourished by the escapee
Grown in the soil of fear
Boiling with anger
Marinated in prejudice
Dripping with desire
Seasoned with selfishness

Sometimes I forget
I often want many things
And they may not be
Going in the same direction
Humming the same tune
Walking the same path
Digging the same hole
Singing from the same hymn-sheet
Ploughing the same furrow
Flying in formation.
And that's okay.

Sometimes I forget
What I want
May be wanting.

Apologia Pro Vita Sua

When I was younger I would bow my head in prayer
And ask good God above to guide my way
I'd kneel before the altar with my worries and my cares
And tell him all the highlights of my day

And every Sunday I would head along to Mass
Mum, Dad, brother, sisters by my side
I'd watch the priest and think that I might do that too,
Bless the people, and raise that chalice high

Growing up a Catholic's not a stain upon my soul
Or any sort of crime I should defend
And I can't speak for others, but I'll say this for myself
It wasn't always fear and guilt and blame.
Do to others as you'd have them do to you,
Be generous, be loving, and be kind
All things being equal, well I could have done much worse
Than live life guided by a Risen Christ.

I've learned suspicion of the overzealous word
The violence of insistence for the truth
I've seen my blindness to the ways that I have hurt
Where all my best intentions were no use
And now I wonder if I'll ever work it out
Or if the point is simply letting go
I'll trust my heart to know to listen for the silence
and to bring me where the gentle waters flow

And just because I'm not enraptured any more
It doesn't mean I don't respect what I've been taught
I just don't think I'm qualified to claim my cause is righteous
Or be absolutely sure that there's a God
But I still live a life of wonder
And I still want a life of prayer
Between the lightning and the thunder
I sometimes pray that she'll be there

Song for a Child

How do you tell a four year-old child it's just the way things are,
That change is just the one thing you can't change?
When she doesn't want cute tadpoles to turn into slimy frogs
But she'd be very grateful if you could just rearrange things for her...
If you can growl like a giant or bark like a dog,
Read a story then go back to the start,
You'll earn yourself a posy of dandelions from the giant
And qualify for a place in her heart.

How do tell a four year old child that you've got work to do,
You'd love to stay and play but can't afford to?
When she wants you to be the voice of Sammy the Snake for another
half an hour
And you know in your heart of hearts that you'd really love to...
If you breathe fire like a dragon or meow like a cat
Well, you're off to a pretty good start
You'll earn yourself a posy of daisies from the garden
And qualify for a place in her heart.

And if you say the magic words you know you'll turn crystal balls into
blackbirds
And watch them fly away

And how do you tell a four year old child that we're all born to die,
That every fond goodbye's a step to freedom?
When she's telling you that she loves you as she's wiping the tears
from your eyes
Cause love can conquer all if you just believe it...
If you can laugh through the anger and play through the pain
Finish stories you were hesitant to start
You'll earn yourself a posy of dandelions from the garden
Qualify for a place in her heart,
Qualify for a place in her heart.

Emailing Rachel

Come gather ye round, lend your ears to the sound
Of this story that I will relate
For it tells of my trials and bold tribulations
In efforts to communicate
With a woman of stature, a woman of grace
A woman of fame and renown
The Flower of St. Thomas, the Belle of Toronto
The pride of Los Angeles town.

I was browsing around to find people to contact
A networker ever I be
Using search engines and emailing people
Who keep websites going like me.
I contacted Blue Planet Green Living and more
I contacted the great and the good
In the cause of community and conversation
I made what connections I could.

In the course of my ramblings and searchings and dabblings
To this page my attention did bend
It said Rachel McAdams the Hollywood actress
She ran a green website with friends
It was called Green Is Sexy, 'twas right down my street
Listing whosits and whatsits galore
So I found her on Facebook and dropped her a line
Never thinking I'd hear any more.

I said that her website was very inspiring
And helped me to rethink my own
It was friendly and colourful, clear and informative
Also decidedly fun,
I never expected I'd get a reply
But a short while had passed when I did
It was short, it was sweet, it was signed "Rachel M."
And she thanked me for what I had said.

Well I joined all the rest of the people on Facebook
Keeping up with her status reports
Olympics and skating, fundraising for Haiti
Backstage from the Oscars, of course;
I sent her a piece that Neil Gaiman had written
That mentioned he'd stepped on her dress.
She replied saying thank you, and sent me a link
To the photographed moment, no less.

Well, I'd have to admit I'm a bit of a fan
Though they wasted her in Sherlock Holmes
She was better in Red Eye in fear of her life
State of Play, or the bold Family Stone
And her turn in The Lucky Ones passed critics by
When I thought she was par excellence
So I told her as much in an email one morning
And hit the send button at once.

For six months I emailed,
not every day, maybe once every three or four weeks,
I was sure she was busy but glad she replied
For the colour it brought to my cheeks.
I was sure to tell friends I was 'emailing Rachel'
And she seemed to be terribly nice
Now, namedropping's not the most subtle of skills
But neither the deadliest vice.

Well at last came the day that her status report
Proclaimed that she'd give it a rest
She was tiring of Facebook, would delete the account
And wished all her fans all the best
Well, I'd emailed her contacts for people I knew
From North and the South, East and West
And so that she'd not lose the info I'd sent
I compiled it all into a list.

I sent the list straight to her friends at the website
Explaining the context, of course
I said I'd emailed the info to Rachel on Facebook
And was now ensuring it wouldn't get lost

Her friend emailed back,
undoubtedly wary of weirdos who're chancing their arm
She said 'Rachel has never had a profile on Facebook'
And sounded the weirdo alarm.

So come all of ye internet ramblers and networkers
Take ye a warning by me
Don't go assuming the profile on Facebook is really the person you see
And should their inventions besmirch your intentions
And leave you with egg on your face
You might meet more people
In face-to-face meetings
Instead of in virtual space.

Once Alien Here

Once alien here
Once alien there
A little bit of a foreigner everywhere
But the truth is I'm tired
I'm looking round at all those people
That I most admire
Getting on with the business of being true
Just like you

Once thrilled by the sky
I'd say I'd felt exhilaration
That I can't deny
Reaching heights that I thought I'd never dare
With eyes open wide
Maybe clearest vision says there is no other side
Could be simple as learning how to care
Being there

Water run and catch the light
A gentler love will guide me through the night
Wake the candle, feed the light
A humbler love will keep me right

Once alien here
Once alien there
Standing still simply left me running scared
But the truth is I'm tired
Of moving on
Addiction to the neophyte's desire
Could be time for the patience for being true
Just like you

Water run and catch the light
A humbler love will guide me through the night
Wake the candle, feed the light
A gentler love will keep me right

The lament of Chicken Little

They say it's not love
If it isn't both ways
And it was
But that's not enough
When the fear is greater than the loss
When the words of bold confusion
Set the scene for hope's regret
When the lure of love's illusion
Can't bridge distance
Can't forget
Mere insistence goes no further
Than an argument well met

They say time heals
But I sometimes wonder if it will
Or will frustration yield
To that Sisyphus fella
With his rolling stone and that tempting hill
When the blindness of perception
Will not let me lay the wreath
On the site of past deception.
Too much guessing
Too much grief
Twisted blessings of the tendency
To lean towards belief

They say it's not love
If it isn't both ways
And it was
But that's not enough
When the fear is greater than the loss
When you make the hard decision
As you pronounce the case adjourned
Make the break with clean precision
You're not helping, lesson learned
Move away before forgiveness
Loses out to bridges burned

Sky falls down
I catch it
I stretch to hang and patch it.
I will not greet the darkness,
I will not douse the flame
I will not raise the anchor,
though the wind is hungry for my sails

Long enough on the island
(for Paul Hogan)

Long enough on the island.
The sun at first did slake our thirst
For urgency to sweep away the darkness.
But chapped lips and burning feet
Revealed the water's invitation.

And so we moved from contemplation
Of coconuts' jewelled hearts and dewy palms
To render trunks as rafts
And offer bark to barnacles.
With cut and thrust we chopped and binded
Till we splashed and splished
With hopes and hearts on far horizons.

Then it happened.

Our hearts so light did lift us up,
Our raft asunder,
Our bodies all in flight,
Till in sun we soaked our skins,
And the sun we became,
The island we became.

Cleaning windows

I'll never know what's even worthwhile learning
If I understand it all too soon
And I won't see all the bridges I've been burning
Till my journey shows me I'm a fool

My life gets bigger or my life gets smaller
It depends on all the courage that I find
And I won't discover all the lands worth seeking
Till I've been at sea a long, long, long, long time

They say the wisdom is all out there somewhere
If I can learn to tell my love from my desire
I crave the balance of the love and the hurting
Of the warmth and the burning of the fire

If I knew where I was going to fall I would lay down a carpet
If I keep trying to pin it down
I'll never know where my heart is

I spend my life cleaning windows
One pane at a time

Roger the Miller (trad.) / Roger the Killer

Young Roger the miller went courting one day
To a farmer's fine daughter named beautiful Kate
She had for her fortune all many fine things
Beautiful silks and gold, diamonds and rings
Her father, he gave her a neat plot of ground
She had also a fortune, she had also a fortune
of five hundred pounds

Well the money and supper, they both were laid down
And it made a great sight to see five hundred pounds
The sight of that money and beauty likewise
Made Roger's heart greedy and dazzled his eyes
He said, "Now that your money and daughter are here
'Tis I will not have her, 'tis I will not have her
without that grey mare"

Well, the money and supper were taken from sight
And likewise young Kathy, his own heart's delight
and Roger was taken and shown out the door
And ordered for not to come there anymore
'Twas then he did tear at his long yellow hair
Saying, "I wish I had never, I wish I had never
spoke of that grey mare"

Now it happened when six months were over and past
Young Roger the miller, he met with this lass
"I think I do know you then, madam," says he
"I am the same way with you, sir," says she
"A man of your features and long yellow hair
He once came a-courting, he once came a-courting
my father's grey mare"

"Well, it was not a-courting the grey mare I came
But you, my own jewel, my Kathy by name
I thought that your father would never dispute
To give me the grey mare along with you to boot
And not to risk lose such a dutiful son

Oh 'tis now I am sorry, 'tis now I am sorry
for what I have done"

"For your sorrow, young Roger, I have little regard
For there's plenty fine men in this town to be had
If you'd forgot the mare, you'd be married, you see
But now you have neither the grey mare nor me
The price of that mare, it was never so great
So, fare thee well, Roger, So fare thee well, Roger,
you're a sorrowful case"

Now Roger's away in his desolate home
And he sighs as he sits there and sups all alone
Kathy, she sings, she is merry and gay
She has wed the young baker who works the long day
So, lads, when you're courting, be always aware
To court with the young maid, to court with the young maid
and not the gray mare

However...

Young Roger the Killer was a born psychopath
He'd been brought up on showerscenes and blood in the bath
But he had a wee problem he daren't overcome
He was agoraphobic and never left home
Young Roger had never been outside his door
Ah, but that didn't stop him, no that didn't stop him
From dreaming of gore.

Well he surfed on the internet all night and day
Indulging his quirks in unusual ways
He plastered newsclippings all over his wall
And scheduled an hour a day just for crank calls
He'd an arsenal of weapons stashed there in his drawer
And he knew exactly, yes he knew exactly
What each one was for.

He had daggers and knives that could stab, cut, and chop
He had poisons enough to make elephants drop
He had shotguns and pistols and rifles galore

Ten poisonous snakes and a circular saw
It's amazing what mail order catalogues sell
He'd a black widow spider, a black widow spider
And Semtex as well.

He thought that his life was a tad unfulfilled
With unsatisfied checklists of people to kill
For want of a person he practised on rats
Insects and mice, spiders, lizards and bats
He was close to his parents whatever he did
With his Mum in the freezer, his Mum in the freezer
His Dad in the fridge.

He'd picked out his victims from all round the town
Dreamt of strangling and dangling them all upsidedown
The schoolteacher, fireman, the baker, the priest
Would all play a part in his sick psycho feast
It was then he did tear at his long yellow hair
Saying "I wish I could leave here, I wish I could leave here,
it's simply not fair!"

So young Roger's away in his desolate home
And he sighs as he sits there and sups all around
In his dreams he decapitates, slices, and peels
Asphyxiates, amputates, never for real
So lads if your bloodlust is brutal and clear
If you're agoraphobic, if you're agoraphobic
Choose a different career.

At the Foot of the Cross

He wanted to watch with the eyes of a child
But he wanted to walk through the night
He wanted to speak with the wisdom of one
Who had opened his arms to the light
And he climbed mountains of love and mountains of hate
Through valleys he travelled with paper cup smiles
And a semi-disposable face

He wanted to fall at the foot of the cross
But he couldn't let go of the rope
He was left writing messages deep in the sand
And the tide came and read what he wrote
And he sailed oceans of love and oceans of hate.
He crossed polished puddles in paper-cup hopes
Just to end up in any old place

He wanted to rescue the tears from the tower
But his sword was too heavy to hold
He danced in his heart with the child in his eyes
To the truth that would never be known
And he walked deserts of love and deserts of hate
Embracing the stones of the wind and the wave
With his fingers that yearned to create

And he tried falling in line
But falling will hurt you if you're falling blind
And he tried marching in time
But time poses questions for linear minds
Gift turns to threat as the future unwinds
Windblown and crying for shelter and dreams
Running from silence and locked away screams
Wondering what in God's name it all means

After the deluge

My father's eyes they spoke of morning's glory
Just when it looked like the deluge would never end
And my mother's eyes they spoke with all the relish of an untold story
Coming round the bend.

And my mother's smile it spoke with warmth and longing
Just when it looked like the waiting would never go
And my father's eyes they spoke of all the burdens
that had lifted from their shoulders
And tumbled far below

And heaven only knows when tides will turn and call the ships to sea
And timeless are the eyes that set the loving hearts free

Will you meet me at the crossroads of my life?
The voyage is long but the winds still blow
when the day has turned to night
And will you stay with me till dark has turned to light
And hold me in the silence of your sight?

My parents lives they speak of love and giving
Of sacrifice for family and for faith
And my parents lives they speak of lessons learned
and strength to battle through the living
Of these true love is made.

And heaven only knows when tides will turn and call the ships to sea
And timeless are the eyes that set the loving hearts free

Will you meet me at the crossroads of my life?
The voyage is long but the winds still blow when the day has turned
to night
And will you stay with me till dark has turned to light
And hold me in the silence of your sight?

Aftermath of an Embassy Reception (Madrid, 1993)

When I head home to tread upon
The hair-trigger of historical remembrance
With words of second-hand wisdom
I shall laugh and recall the evening that we
Raised our lives on cocktail sticks,
Dipped in the explanatory sauce, the
Glorious self-deprecation and practised regret
Of the (temporary) Northern Irish
Irish exile,
Leaning on the shadows of a setting sun that
Dangles with bloodshot sighs above
My days of presumed abandon.

Somewhere a bomb etches slow-motion into a
Granite gravestone
To the invitation of a bullet
Drawn by the gravity of
Unique problematic complexity
While quiet, cup of tea desperation
Drips slowly from the tired wounds
To stain our streets like Judas rain of
Fashionable apathy.

Hell, hate, and high water
Provide pleasant conversation
At an Embassy reception
As the pseudo-sage seeks to rear his head once more.
So I raise my hand
Striking the death blow
In the name of vain pursuits
With the natural ease of one who lives
Where red is just another colour on the kerbstone.

Side to side

I have no faith in progress, evolution, or in fate
It's we that make our histories as our histories, too, are made
And I have no faith in power, if we only mean control
For the power to be gentle is a power we can know

And I have no faith in meaning if we only mean our own
The more we fix our meanings, the more we feel alone
And I've no faith in intuition, if it means I'm walking blind
I'd rather be uncertain, than be convinced I'm always right

I have no faith in contracts, if they're built on lack of trust
I'd rather think I'd like to, I wouldn't like to think I must
But it helps to have faith sometimes, helps to have a guiding star
And I'd like to celebrate you, for the person that you are

And I danced with you on beaches
Beneath the moon on starry nights
And I know I learned to love you
And I hoped I always might
And dancing with you was easy
And that's usually a good sign
So we danced away the moonlight
Swaying gently, side to side

And oh, round and round we go
Look me in the eyes and I will know
And oh, round and round we go
hold me close and dance with me real slow

The poltergeist rap!

I'm Hector the spectre
the ghost with the most
I'm the phantom with the banter
I'm the scary at your bedpost
the one to wake you screaming
when you're trying to have a nap
I'm the quality purveyor of
the poltergeist rap!

I'm the ghoulie in the white sheet
the moaner in the hood
the dangler of the chains
the little ghost who could
I'm the creaking in the corridor
the dripping from the tap
I'm the quality purveyor of
the poltergeist rap!

Well I've seen the worst of mediums
their clichés and their tedium
I really have been mean to them
I've even made them cry
do their best to deceive
you believe every message you receive as you grieve
find it hard to say goodbye

You can track me with your knowledges
Your experts and technologies
Your parapsychologies, your EMF machines
But from coast to coast I'm the ghost with the most
From Rosenheim in Germany to Borley Rectory

I'm the spirit who's the loudest
I'm the scariest and proudest
I'm the phantom who's the rowdiest
The poltergeist king
Just know that I can see ya

With your tables and your ouija
I bet I'm gonna freak ya
Gonna make you sing!

It's the smashing, the dashing
The lashings of dramatic flair and passion
That keep me at the top of my game
It's the plates, the dishes
I tell ya it's delicious when the knocking and the rumbling
Brings the fear and the fame!

I'm Hector the spectre
the ghost with the most
I'm the phantom with the banter
I'm the scary at your bedpost
The one to wake you screaming
When you're trying to have a nap
I'm the quality purveyor of
The poltergeist rap!

I'm the ghoulie in the white sheet
The moaner in the hood
The dangler of the chains
The little ghost who could
I'm the creaking in the corridor
the dripping from the tap
I'm the quality purveyor of
The poltergeist rap!

Learn

I never really gave myself the chance to love you truly
Sort of like a hug without the full embrace
Maybe I was scared that my heart would be unruly
Maybe I was scared that you'd see my only face

Maybe I lost trust in the beauty of the moment
Maybe I lost trust in the beauty that was you
I'm feeling kind of stupid now that I can see the chances
Where I could have learned the wisdoms of a love so bright and new

I'm kind of glad that you're not me
But I'd like to learn you.

When the quest for explanations leaves a tiredness in my answers
When the silence of the heart will leave a tiredness in my eyes
When I leave a space for difference in the hope that's where the dance
is
And somewhere in the dancing's where I finally realise

I'm kind of glad that you're not me
But I'd like to learn you.

If I sacrifice the answers to the wonder of unknowing
If I listen to your voice instead of waiting for my say
If I loosen up my grip on the patterns of the future
Even if it means that I decide to walk away

I'm kind of glad that you're not me
But I'd like to learn you.

Frankenstein's Monster

Frankenstein's Monster was having a bad, bad day
It really was sad to see him that way
Out of luck and all out of dreams, he was coming apart at the seams
Frankenstein's Monster was having a bad, bad day

Frankenstein's Monster was having a bad, bad day
He had tried putting pieces together in a logical way
But his attempts to climb out of bed had cost him an arm and a leg
Frankenstein's Monster was having a bad, bad day

Frankenstein's Monster was having a bad, bad day
He put his best foot forward, but it just came away
It puts a big strain on your heart when your whole life is falling apart
Frankenstein's Monster was having a bad, bad day

Frankenstein's Monster was having a bad, bad day
He still had plenty to do and plenty to say
But the stories that he would have told were now but a jaw to behold
Frankenstein's Monster was having a bad, bad day

Frankenstein's Monster was having a bad, bad day
When someone's life is in bits there's not much you can say
Of all of the things that are known, chances are that you'll rip what
you've sewn
Frankenstein's Monster was having a bad, bad day

Untitled #2

Rush in slush
Rhymes cold with wet

Slow in snow
Rhymes cold with transcendental meditation

Stand beside the one you love
(for Clare and Ross)

Stand beside the one you love
Thank the stars for their intentions
Raise a glass that with your loving hearts you'll walk together
Knowing you've more than enough
Knowing even when it's rough
You're there beside the one you love

Stand beside the one you love
Smile at how it came to happen
Raise a glass that with your loving hearts you'll work together
Everything will be okay
Loving hearts can guide the way
Stand beside the one you love

And when it's hard just wait it out
Give it time you'll see it through
Learn to listen for what loving's all about
When you're standing with the one who's loving you

Stand beside the one you love
Bless the day and bless the hour
Raise a glass that with your loving hearts you'll dream together
Live the hope that bears you up
When it's easy, when it's tough
Stand beside the one you love

And when it's hard just wait it out
Give it time you'll see it through
Learn to listen for what loving's all about
When you're standing with the one who's loving you

Everything will be okay
Loving hearts can guide the way
Stand beside the one you love

Sasquatch Symposium (Vancouver, 1998)

Twas down by the forests of bush, bird and tree
in those groves of delight in Vancouver B.C.
That a fine merry band of the great and the good
did gather for Harvey's debate, oh!
For many's a day and for many's a year
they had stood up to danger and stood up to fear,
They did ford raging rivers and cross raging seas
at the bold invitation of fate, oh!

For the source of their quest was unquenchable thirst,
whether research be good, bad, indifferent or worse,
Yes their quest was no less than to track down the beast
that did spurn their endeavours and trials, oh!
For of all of the creatures of forest and lake,
be they lions or tigers or venomous snake,
There is none so elusive of fame grand and great
than bold Big Foot, that wild hairy man, oh.

He's been witnessed by thousands big, middlin' and small,
sure there's some say he's bruisin', full thirteen feet tall,
There's some sure they'll swear they saw nothing at all,
till purses are filled for the tale, oh!
There's some say they've played hours of peekety-boo
with a creature that most would consign to a zoo,
There's some say he speaks telepathically too,
with fine words he would chat and persuade, oh.

Then there's some say he's more a time traveller of sorts,
a paradimensional user of vortices,
Travellin' with aid of those grand UFOs,
those fine flying saucers so rare, oh!
Sure he'll pop up in front of you out of the blue,
then he'll leave without warning or how do you do,
And you're left there to wonder illusion or true,
with your jaw hanging open for flies oh!

Well, Franzoni was there with his placenames and lore,

citing Skookums and Cultus and Devils galore
By all of these names they knew Sasquatch before
in First Nations' parlance and talk, oh.
There were Almas and Momos and Splintercats too,
and Yetis and Yowees with Ditjeridus
Wild Men and Wild Women they make up the crew
of hairy relations and friends, oh.

There was Strasenburg, Pye, Cotton, Bradshaw and Kirk,
Lapseritis and Steenburg and Herriot's smirk
Bindernagel and Milner, Dahinden and Page,
Seepeetza and bold Paul le Blond, oh!
There was Neiss, there was Green, Krantz and Fahrenbach too,
(and Kokanee Beer they did sponsor the do)
And Erik the Viking who stormed out of view
with sparks flying out of his hair, oh!

There were books, there were pamphlets of every sort,
with pictures of things that have never been caught,
There were stickers and cups, t-shirts all to be bought
by the cryptozoologists there, oh.
And we must not forget Roger Patterson's flick,
it's been a good many years and the air it's still thick
with the arguments, details that all contradict,
Bluff Creek certainly seems aptly named, oh.

So come all of you ramblers wherever you be,
if it's Big Foot you're after just head to B.C.
Where the forests are filled with the bird, bush and tree
and plenty of space to get lost, oh!
And if you should happen to meet one of them,
sure say "How's it goin'? I come as a friend!
Have you ever considered the fine dividends
that come in publicity's wake, oh?"

But you'll find that the Sasquatch is shy as they come -
you'll see hide nor hair if you're carrying a gun or a
Camera you'll end up with evidence none
to prove that the skeptics are wrong, oh.
But you'll smell lots of smells and you'll hear lots of screams

and the Big Foot and Yeti will haunt all your dreams
But you're welcome next year in Granville B.C.
at the Sasquatch Symposium there, oh!

Chance would be a fine thing

I never thought I'd find someone to share my love of zombies
Someone who knows that garlic won't keep vampires from our door
Someone who'll come in handy when we're being attacked by were-
wolves
Someone who has a library full of supernatural lore

I never thought I'd find someone with such a love of sci-fi
Battlestar Galactica, (early) Star Wars, Doctor Who
Someone who doesn't mind we'll name our children after starships
Someone for whom each rerun always feels like something new

I never thought I'd find someone with a heart so lovely
I never thought an angel would come knocking at my door
A smile so full of kindness, a love so soft and gentle
A heart there to remind me just what my grace is for

I never thought I'd find someone so many kinds of awesome
Every day's for dancing with her beauty by my side
I wake and watch her sleeping and I know I truly love her
And I know that that's forever with the love I feel inside

Chance would be a fine thing, to find someone who loves me
Chance would be a fine thing, a love so rare and true
Chance would be a fine thing, someone who actually sees me
Chance would be a fine thing, it is, and I found you

About Anthony

Anthony McCann is an experienced ethnomusicologist, anthropologist, and folklorist. As a freelance journalist and broadcaster he has written for The Irish Times and Hot Press Magazine, and won a SONY award for community radio as a presenter/producer with Strule FM in 2009. Notably, he worked as Assistant Coordinator of the 1999 UNESCO / Smithsonian World Conference on the "Safeguarding of Traditional Culture and Folklore". He currently holds the position of Research Associate with the Smithsonian Center for Folklife and Cultural Heritage. His academic honours have included a Fulbright Award and the Charles Seeger Prize for ethnomusicology.

Ordering Information

To order additional copies of this book (either in bulk or individual sales), please email orders@clarionpublishing.com, and give the title, author, and ISBN number, along with any additional details relating to your enquiry. We will be happy to assist you.

clarion
PUBLISHING

CPSIA information can be obtained at www.ICGtesting.com
Printed in the USA
BVOW071053240512

291025BV00003B/1/P